Poetry by
Gloria Wimberley

Dialect
Of
Dahlias

Edgar & Lenore's Publishing House
13547 Ventura Boulevard
Sherman Oaks CA 91423
www.EdgarAllanPoet.com

Dialect of Dahlias
Gloria Wimberley © 2012
All rights reserved.

No part of this publication may be reproduced, stored in a retrieval system or transmitted by any means without expressed written consent by publisher and/or author.

Printed in the United States of America

Poetry written by Gloria Wimberley
Foreword and editing by Apryl Skies
Co-editing by Alicia Winski
Cover design by Apryl Skies & Gloria Wimberley

ISBN-13: 978-0985471507
ISBN-10: 0985471506
Library of Congress Control Number: 2012937577

Dedications

~

To my mini-muses, Shea (6) & Lizanna (3);

my font of support, David;

and my parents, David and Karen McGowan,

who live in my heart's home:

(Almost Heaven, West Virginia),

for always believing in me

~

…Also, dedicated to the memory

of my beloved

Grandmother Mae "DewBee" McGowan

&

my dear friend Tammi "T-Rose" Evans

~

Foreword by Apryl Skies

Gloria Wimberley's debut poetry collection, *"Dialect of Dahlias"*, presents a uniquely rich balance of color and shadow. This bewitching collection of poetic artistry features a series of poems, both stylistic and intriguing. With a focus on structure, whimsy and wordplay, Wimberley's approach to language is artful and dynamic.

As a shy and (pen)sive child, Wimberley found her voice by writing with character and curiosity. The poems included in this tome explore the world through a creative and inspiring perspective.

Divided into two distinct chapters to highlight opposing tone and style, the first chapter *Lilies* showcases a hopeful and heartfelt embrace on life in all its fear and fascination. Unfolding the many facets of experience, Wimberley begins her recount speaking from beneath the blackberry bushes as a series of storytelling poems paint a portrait of living in the lush, kelly-green hills of West Virginia.

The symbolic chapter *Lepers* is methodical; written with dramatic repose, enigma and intensity. This sequence of poems is particularly in-depth and expressed through a more shrouded vernacular and vibration. Each measure is layered and thematic using intentional idiosyncratic sway and decadent metaphor.

The pairing of these two chapters is *sui generis* and indeed a testament to Wimberley's craft as a poet. This deeply imaginative contrast sets the bar high for contemporary poetry in that her voice remains undefined, showing no sign of limitations.

Wistful, wise and wicked are the words of Gloria Wimberley and the poetry within this collection will enchant and recant the theory that *poetry is dead...*

True lovers of literature will find *"Dialect of Dahlias"* more intoxicating with each read.

"...Flower

        of an adding

where

       a follower..."

from

Hotel Francois 1er

by Gertrude Stein

Table of Contents
P(art) I: Lilies

Escape from the Crow Cage	10
(What is) Before Me	11
The Shortest Reign in OurStory	12
Of Clouds and Clarity	13
Wind Jockeys	14
My Favorite Old Lady	16
100 Degrees in the Shade	17
Grandma in Her Prime	19
Dawnlily in a Bailiwick	20
Sequoias	21
Wishblue	22
Manatee & Monet	23
Westercheck Girl, aka my student Wendy	24
Forgiveness on the Tongue	25
Of Grandmothers and Grace	26
Petalpink Fanfare	28
Motes of Motherhood	29
Sepia & Song	30
Shimmer of Dragonflies	31
Bewitching Baby: Miss Liz at Midnight	32
Jar o' Jellybean @ 20 months	33
Poem for my Daughters	34
Pieces of a Liquid Puzzle	35
Subtlety	36
A Day for Shea	37
Silver Silver…Alice Blue	38
Mama Wearies then Brightens	39
A Mountain Mama Remembers	40

P(art) II: Lepers

Musemagik	42
Swill o'Swain	43
Thistlethink	44
Cotillion Eye Glinting Down	45
Thoughts trickling before sleep	46
Self As Sea	47
Swan Junket	48

Taproot	49
Lovecrest	50
Chameleon Under a Black Rainbow	51
Bloom~of~the~Womb	52
Blood Bloom	53
Abby and Me: A.D	54
Giana in the Wheat	56
Arinna	57
Ruth	58
Burnt Offering	60
MoonMince	61
My Butterflies After Midnight	62
He	63
Posies & Pyres	64
Kaiser Kiss	66
Satori in a Bell Jar	67
Honkytonk Heartbreak	68
Calico Roses in a Skull Vase	70
Moon's Metal	71
Gypsy Crescendo	72
L'oncle-In-Law	74
Pere Heirs	76
Echoes of Adam	77
Black Lily: A Slight Incantation	78
Breezy Green Limbo	79
London Son	80
Banshee Breeze	81
An Iris View	82
IDiotica	83
Filmmakers	84
Digital Swan	85
La Danse de Vie	86
Cantomine	87
MetroGnome	88
Blue Room, Red Room	89
Revelation	90
A Woman's Face	91
To Think Askance	92
Eyes Flashin' Ashen	93
Anomalily	94
About the Author	96
Acknowledgments	98

P(art) 1: Lilies

"Hope is the thing with feathers -
That perches in the soul -
And sings the tune - without the words-
And never stops - at all -..."

~"Hope" by Emily Dickinson

Escape from the Crow Cage

Shyness is a shell
I live in
my voice locked
in a yolk of whys

Only you...
jacinth of the sunrise
can give my voice wings—
let me break out
of the invisible impasse
let my heart breathe again—
red ~ alive ~ untrussed...

Once free,
I will not look back
like Lot's wife
I will be a pearly, black pillar
of
bloodflesh
and freedompulse...
once out
in the honeyed sunlight

--reach for me

With wings spread
I am dancing
on a broken shell now, friend
--don't
make
me
go
back

(What is) Before Me

Awaking to this dream shred:
a hand-sized rectangular panel
falling from my grasp...
a sheer of grey...
it could be
silk, satin, or thinnest velvet
It could be a remembrance of sky
--grey, cold, windy--
connected
to a child's recollection
of a soul-cozy Thanksgiving Day
in West Virginia...

What it is
is a swatch of mind
fabric mine:
so gossamer, yet stiff and sticky
like briars in the now-winterbarren
"Blackberry Heaven" of my childhood
that catch on a woolen coat,
those jagged briarfingers
that draw a ragged line of blood
on wind-chapped skin
as hunting dogs (beagles)
bark while scampering through staid woods
In this dreamscape also stand
tiny arms of black flower petals...
a pig-tailed girl's rendition of
ashen daisies in abstract
on a soft swatch of kimono sleeve
grey silk
that becomes a delicate reminder
of night-sky vistas decorated with pixie-painted stars
stitched silver by Mother

Memory
~the only real thread
I can
hold onto

The Shortest Reign in OurStory

I remember
Heide, Freddy, Alan, and me
frolicking through sun-speckled woods
playing tag, and hide & go seek then
--TIMEOUT--
(squinting, sunburnt faces
slurping cherry Kool-Aid for "energy")

Our Play resumes
with Reality as an unwelcome playmate:
a wide-eyed, dirt-stained face
cut finger…tiny drop of blood
drips into the summer dust…
as poignant as a piano plink
but is soon forgotten in the Gamecommotion
Until the waning afternoon rays
mark the end of our Day
(the End of Play)
and the Mothervoices called us home.
I remember the realm of Play
where Childhood was king
and Imagination was queen

vive la reine[1]

---

[1] *Vive la reine* = "Long live the queen" in French

Of Clouds & Clarity

A veil of smoky blue velvet
lifts in my mind
to waft out wispy
motes of memories:
My grandmother's smoke-rings
formed an ethereal nimbus
above her sister's head...

In the nearby dimly-lit living room,
I watched the life-is-perfect Brady Bunch
on TV in the 70's,
they laughed & chatted,
sipped beer in the afternoon,
smoked Salems,
played Yahtzee for hours,
sat in uncomfortable, metal chairs
in a cramped kitchen
--never complained
about simple, yet satisfying lives
in the kelly-green hills of Appalachia
(a small Brickyard Bend town in West Virginia)

Even when my oft-lucid great-aunt
joked and smiled through
an especially trying MS haze
~~a plume of plaintiveness
rising in Bobby Vinton's voice
on the radio as he crooned,

She wore bluuuuuueeee velvet...

Their sun-burnished glint
of silver lining never turned dark
never turned ashen grey

Wind Jockeys

We shared a Polish grandma
Helen
who smoked too much
while playing Yahtzee with Great-Aunt Julia
--both were addicted to Bobby Vinton
who crooned in the background…smoky velvet

As cousins
we shared a steep green hill
that leaned toward heaven
--while we sloppily chalked our names
on an uneven black rock
moss-grounded baby crag
--where we carved our initials
on trees rooted in that hill

JB GM

Every summer
our family scurried like piss-ants
(also called sugar ants) at a picnic
as my 'Nam-numbed uncle
with his green
"Born Free" tattoo
slapped meat patties on the hissing bbq grill
and cursed that heat
(the sticky heat that glues pores shut)
as Jen-Jeff-Bry-and I
romped with the overt ladybugs
and the covert ticks in the tiny yard
--not a one being content with the grassy cage
but Jen and I were content
with a child's dreamday:
nibbling Fig Newtons in the elfin broom-closet in the kitchen
twirling like human tops
while blaring, "Wonder Womaaannnnn"
giggling superheroines high on Pixy Stix
yet we yearned to climb that hill—

"to scale the mountain"

to see for ourselves—Grandma's myth:
wild horses floating
on clouds of earth
in a corral caressing the edge of the woods…

She warned us never to go there:
"too dangerous for little girls"
…but following our cantering hearts
we quickly crawled over moss, fern, and anthill
past our initialed tree
and autographed stone
That Day, we almost reached the top
holding our breath
while listening through the breeze
we could hear
the harmony of hoofbeats,
the symphony of whinnysong

--But Grandma's voice climbed air,
reigning us back
long-faced, we left our bit
of magic in its cloud of dust
and crawled away from our tree, our stone
our horses in an ivory corral
back to smoky
blue velvet

Standing in the green swatch called "yard"
with the ladybugs and ticks
having been gently branded "bad" for the day
Jen & I both knew
why the horses floating in clouds of dust
like us were not born free either

My Favorite Old Lady

As my West-by-God Granny liked to say:
"She don't get around much anymore — that odd-turned old lady…"

She'd growl when strangers
poked around the house
set on the edge of the woods
she'd hide behind the green
bushes and even nap in the shade
"when the spirit moved her"
and when I stepped over the low
stone wall on the edge of the bank to meet her
her mood grew especially merry
and being her best friend, I couldn't be happier;
Miss Tippy's smile
has always been the sun to me…

Our favorite friend-ritual:
to walk a "country mile" around a sprawling
blackberry field rounded by oaks, maples, and birches
(even though she's been hobbled by rheumatism
for the last few last years now)
straying from the worn path
she'd wander into Queen Anne's lace
wade into a sea of buttercups,
which made her playful, alive
kissed by the sun
--not like me on the trodden trail
shaded by the outstretched arms of trees
I, alone, have understood this odd-turned lady
our secret language as natural as rain to rose
yet tears turned to rain
when this *grand dame* with her sleek black egghead
and brown M&M eyes ringed white with age
died…

For sixteen human years
she was my "baby girl"
but the neighbors, in their darkness, whisper:

"There she goes — visiting that spaniel's grave again."
I just sprinkle buttercups and Queen Anne's lace
where Tippy lies buried in a patch of sun
in our Blackberry Heaven

100 Degrees in the Shade

At the Turn of the Century Festival
in Weirton, West Virginia,
a gap-toothed
honey-haired
teenage boy
stands by his family's wares;
he wears
a gone fishin' straw hat

When the man
in the Armani suit
approaches---points---impatiently
thrusts out
a crisp fifty-dollar-bill,
the boy humbly hands
to the man, his baby--
a buck knife
painstakingly scrimshawed
with the design of an intricate
clipper ship floating in
delicate black lines
sailing on a sea
of bone…

When the man curtly asks
for change,
the boy says with a stammer
(eyes lowered)
"I-I can't count…
Let me get my Ma"

Seeing the boy's face redden
in that already merciless
August heat
makes the man
shuffle uncomfortably
know Shame

--feel its scarlet blade--

Grandma in Her Prime

"Oh, wasn't he handsome, sweetie?
My, if you could've seen us then..."

    With a wish and a sigh
      swish of a
   sailor suit and a polka dot dress
 swaying
  to the sexy slur of a saxophone
     and torrid trumpet
    bass throbs
  as her brunette head bobs
 in the ballroom
Smoky white sequin-glints
 sashay clockwise
  across a hardwood floor
    He — with his sandy brown hair
   slicked back
   leads gingerly
  She — with her Betty Boop eyes
coy lash-action (then sweet laughter)
   to his satisfaction…
    Tender is the butterfly touch
     of a silhouette kiss
       clarinet trills to a climax
        as the smoky white glints
         of diamonds dance over the lovers:
       This began
       their foxtrot
      of 43 years…

    Smiling, I started to hand the worn
   snapshot to Grandma
    but she wasn't there
      While I stood
       holding her memory
       she was lost in a reverie
      flirting and foxtrotting
     once again
~dancing with Grandpa in his prime

Dawnlily in a Bailiwick

Today I learned that Life is an egg
(ambergris and cracked)
as my mother's cousin Sunshine
lay in a hospital bed--in a coma
from diabetic shock

Her husband of many years, George,
fought to recover from the godshock of it all…
he squeezed her hands and stroked her pale face
as the machines breathed on schedule
in cruel harmony

Tears crawled from his bloodshot eyes
as he prayed for a miracle
a quickening, a life-ebb

Night-shift nurses shook their heads
and shuffled down the corridor…away
a miracle seemed a rotting wives' tale,
but the echoes of sobs followed them

Exhausted, George cradled Sunshine's hand
in the grey light of the hospital room
--wishing that he could kill
the machines' rhythmic sighing
--hoping that his heartbeat did not die
as hers began wilting from within
yet he held his breath and waited…for a flicker
waited…for
waited for his Sunshine / to break through the fragile wall
and into the peaceful embrace
of the lilied light

Sequoias...
for S.F.R.

Once red sentinels:
tree titans
of sylvan
peace:
reduced to two blocks
of wood…

(we) communing in whispers
mouthpiece of wind
time split us cleanly

Will the blinding light
of His blade ever dim?

She and I
sitting on a split-rail
fence
--no pioneer past
to pack a pipe
and smoke about
by stout men, with
sun-etched crows' feet
coveting their contemplative
chin-scratching,
pea-
cock posturing
and broad cowboy stances
in the dust

In this Dust
of the Land
that wind-whispers
our names
long after the men's pipes
have been fossilized
in the bowels
of Mother Earth

Wishblue

She says Life is...

sleeping like a stone
stained-glass keeper
etched in the brain
coral that eschews
the ghostly blue
sting of the man o' war
with his tenter-hook
tentacles silent
in search of flesh
to touch

"Meddy's" eyes ever cast down
to the mysterious depths of indigo
Mere Mer
so inked in myth and tidal pith

Like a mermaid-as-anchor
she sinks
to the water-weighted sand
closing her ethereal blue eyes
to the world...

Ms. Medusa sleeps heavily
--dreaming of touch
without the sting

Manatee and Monet

In the steaming jungles of Mexico
where ghosts of Mayans
bend weeds with wind...as they walk by
--where the furred tarantula
who rears up like a stallion
when it hears that rattle (telltale in the dust)
--where a pack of sun-sheened dogs,
who have adopted, as one of them,
a wild piglet whose mother in her haste, left him behind:
They romp and play as one...

In the blueblack depths
of an underwater cave
revered by natives of Akumal
swims my frogman:
I know he will touch a pale sea anemone of petal pink
with delicacy and respect
"Bonita" he may think;
such pastels never fade
in a Monet landscape
(even underwater)

Later, on land, he compares me
to a mermaid shimmering in an undersea garden
of watercolors. Later still,
as Night ladles blackness over the villa, I wonder if
~my frogman my love~
sees me
after many years of marriage
not as a mermaid...but as a manatee
--After we've both discovered
with a mutual smile...
the comfortable truth in the play of light
...of a Monet landscape

Westercheck Girl
for my Student Wendy

On an ordinary day
in my
otherwise docile
college English classroom,
the calm ends--
--as the familiar storm
air perfumed purple,
as with lilacs
swirls darkly into being:
Westercheck girl
drumming up drama
with her tattooed
pupils
and angry,
freckled
calla lily of a face
…defensively cutting
others with her
shardsharp words
in discussion…in argument
…in passing
Never mincing or wincing
~or waning in strength
in her feckless quest
(to matter)
…reckless unrest
to the cosmic lake o'sip
in the jagged
pool
of her soul
Wordlessly, breathlessly
~spent from the effort of it all
she touches
such a reflection
with fingers of brine

Forgiveness on the Tongue

"What...near my voice"
Zillah thought she heard softly
in a softer head-cloud
of a dream...

Her Kyoko, sultry,
even after their thorntwist aria
of a fight
spoke
focused
and breathy
as a bamboo reed,
which trembles
ever so slightly in
morning's
mouth
of
jade-green mist
and honeyed dew

...how crisp & clean the taste
of mercy

Of Grandmothers & Grace

Tears seal me
in an ice floe,
drown and bury me
in the frozen, snow-bound earth

Tears warm me
with winter
splash me with the refreshing yesterdays
spent with my grand Grandmother "DewBee"…

Nowadays…
"Life is as ugly as a mud fence"
and twice as dark without her,
Life is "colder than Billy Buck"

To Grief
I'd love to bid farewell,
to shout:

"Hey Grief!
You're for the birds — go pound salt!"

O Sorrow
"Go pedal your papers!"
and tell Mourning
that it will have to make do with a
"lick and a promise"
because *Time*
(supposedly) *heals* all wounds

My glacier of pain
is melting
my ice-glazed cocoon
is loosening
my wings of memory and light
are fully-formed and unfolding now
and I intend to

"Go sailin' downtown Weirton"

then sail skyward…above the earth, and the ice, and Fate—

(which can be a "P-R-I-C-K — Prince!")

I am robin-egg blue
and buttercup yellow and deep orange
delicately brushstroked with powdery black accents
~a butterfly the color of "blue muckle dun" she would say

And I am floating on air
alongside my angel-granny
who smiles with the warmth of the sun
because we are together again
in spirit

Our grandmother~granddaughter love
is like the splendor of springtime eternal
then her voice is golden windchimes
on a gentle breeze as she says:

"That's the ber-*RIES*, sweetie!"

because at that moment over the sprawling meadow
and forest-beauty
of Blackberry Heaven, West Virginia
(our hearts' home)
we flutter by and remember
we…flutter…by

PetalPink Fanfare

A voice without volume
speaks without words
in a watery whisper
imperceptible
warbles pianissimo
reverberating with strength
during Life's refrain of sunrise and sunset…

In a heartbeat crescendo
she is calling through the caul
touching this gossamer
membrane with tiny fingers
Within wombwalls of infinite warmth
(a bailiwick of liquid embrace)
she waits…
with the will of a rosebud
for her "window" to her world
to burst open
so she can someday
reach
for the colorsplash of rainbows
the whitedesign of snowflakes
the tender touch of mother's hand…

And now at this particular moment,
she is trumpeting
her existence
--her voice
to be heard at last
letting all who gaze lovingly
and swaddle her snugly
hear Life's triumphant gracenote:

A Baby is Born

Motes of Motherhood

Childbirth in short:
"bowling ball with hair" bursts forth
emerges: pink…loud

Her name means "fairy place"
…no sparkly wings to flutter
the moon still smiles

Toddler thoughts erupt
lava of crayons flow bright
ejecta is art

Leaves, dirt, and grass
heaped on a Cinderella tea-party plate
~~perfect lunch for a babydoll

Butterfly's shadow
dances over my daughter
~~her face is my sun

Childhood flits by on hummingbird wings
camera clicks to catch it
…only memories aflutter in my mother-heart

Sepia & Song

Sepia seeping
into the Perfect Picture
but there's no camera around
to capture
our gentle swaying
in the kitchen
or her baby head lying
warmly on my shoulder
or my arms enveloping her lovingly
as I mint
in my weary mind
this mother-daughter moment…
(Plaintive Scottish fiddle-song on the radio)
hugs us parenthetically
as we continue swaying
silently as one
her tears long since dried,
her eyes long since closed;
her long, dark eyelashes are doll perfection…
As the song lilts to an end,
my own eyes are moist;
I'm wishing
with a mother's wistfulness
that the permanence of sepia
could seep in…
seal us
bond us
in wordless bliss
for a lifetime
of refrains,
not bridges

Shimmer of Dragonflies~~

Undulating
under
the briny-blue
shirt I'm wearing
is her sister
floating
in
a warm womb-sea

…I wish Liz
could see her
Big Sister Shea
(who is actually little)
a 2-year-old
scampering around
the spring-green yard
sun glinting
on her flaxen curls
as she clasps
her hands together
to catch the winged wonders

…but she can only hold air…

Beaming and giggling
as in my belly
her sister
(as if with womb-wings)
is airily wiggling
--like the dragonflies
so shimmery
and elusive

Bewitching Baby: Miss Liz at Midnight

Stirring
within
a cauldron
of
floral-print
cotton,
"bubbles of trouble"
are soon forgotten
Drops
of a "magic potion"
(Mylicon)
along with soothing
words
and soft
rocking
make such
bubbles
BE GONE!!!
…Now-calm,
Baby
smilingly
slips
into sleep
--as
lullabies
are
lilting
and
diaper bags
are
deep

Jar o' Jellybean at 20 months old

Pffffft!

go the deity-
clouds
of powder
when
she
plops,
but her angelic
giggles
are louder…

Lizzi-Lu, Lizzi-Lu
how we savor
smile and coo:
"Michelin-man legs"
marshmallow
--soft, warm
plum-dark
peepers
deeper
than
the eye of the storm
Big Sister's shadow
and *all* of our sun…

Her bright "la-laa…" Smurf song
eclipses din of day…
so shines
the fun

Poem For My Daughters

Winding a blue
sea of swirled green,
black letters,
and an angelfish
tightly around
each of her fingers,
she soon resembles
a baby Bob Cratchit;
the address labels
form minimalist
reverse fingerless gloves
for my 3-year-old daughter Shea

Her laugh: jolly
Her smile:
cheerier than boughs of holly
when she gently kisses
the forehead
of her baby sister Lizzi
whose chin glistens
with teething drool

At that moment
I know
that the ungilded beauty
(pine tree-green, not money-green)
of the season
has ebbed
ocean-like
over me

Pieces of a Liquid Puzzle

Filled her wooden name
puzzle
with jacinth juice
then gingerly poured out the liquid
(to her, a magic elixir)
into a plastic Cinderella
teacup of water
and then back into her empty
puzzle space
(the 4 letters of her name
in primary colors, scattered nearby)

As she sat splayed on towels that lay across the kitchen tile
concentrating on her concoction,
art and alchemy
became birds of the same wing
My baby girl
~ all smiles and purpose
showed me…

We
can fill up our names
our identities
with meaning
no matter how fluid
or murky

Subtlety

Amazing me with such artistry, this
diminuitive "druid"
hooded in pink
terrycloth
studies her "canvas" with
concentration
far beyond her years; she is 3

As still as stone and as deep as a chant at dusk
she draws
a large circle
on the white
dry erase board of her Crayola easel
--no uncertainty announced in wobbly lines
With the patience and introspective silence
of a nuanced master (no smudges or smears)
she retraces with only her small finger
the circle
backwards...rewinding time
slowly and with laser-beam precision
erasing the circle's existence, its
possibility of
being...

a sun, a smileyface, a curved monolith
in snakygreen marker

A Day for Shea

Sky-blue folds of
Cinderella's
dress sweep gracefully
across a "ballroom floor"
of lilac-purple
and lily-white icing

Her golden 'do
upswept in eternal perfection,
her tiny face
illuminated
by 4 petal-pink birthday candles
that stand near the fancy,
matching, pink castle
...as much bigger faces
eagerly crowd
around the party table to sing

(Baby Sister "Jellybean", who is teething, will drool, instead)

while our firstborn daughter
"Peanut"
smiles brightly
and glows
with the happiness of being:

Princess For A Day

Silver Sliver...Alice Blue

A sliver of silence
brings paper-thin
pain...
to quiver
like a hummingbird
caught in
wings of rain
~ ice blue ~

Spark O' Soul

A sprig of pine
ever thine
shan't wilt
from wound of sun
but shrivels from
lack of fairy flame
which warms us--every one

"Mama Wearies then Brightens"

I wanted to bathe
(but instead I bathed in the sun)
I wanted to sweep the floors
but for fun,
I swept away
a stickysilver web
between two trees
and laughing, mused
that I'd hurt no one
Then I saw that because of Me
--and my sun-sudden glee
a hardworking spider
was homeless…

I wanted to tidy up the house
--pick up the books, dolls, and toys
the Dr. Seuss-esque gizmos that bring mirth of noise
…but I preferred subtle joys
'stead of work, I focused on fun:
my child and I played
until the day was done…

Please give my regards to the conspiratorial sun
I don't regret chores undone

A Mountain Mama Remembers

Up Campground Hill in Tomlinson Run State Park, WV
I walk with my husband of 14 years
the view---green tranquility of trees
the incline—satisfyingly steep,
which stretches
my legs…

Meanwhile, I stretch my mind
with memories:
storytelling
while roasting marshmallows
-- over a cozy campfire with family
…catching lightning bugs
in denim-blue twilight
with neighbor-kids

when I was
"…knee-high to a grasshopper"
Grandpa would say
…rocking & talking on the breezy front porch
with my grand Grandma
Her smile and voice,
sweet as dulcimer music
floating on mountain air
"That's the berries!" I say
(as Grandma often would)
as my husband and I reach the hilltop

~~My grandmother's merry saying
is an echo, evergreen
in the Queen Anne's Lace
and blackberry blossoms
of my thriving
memory
garden

P(art) II:
Lepers[2]

"...Cold metal walks across my forehead.
Spiders search for my heart.
It is a light that goes out in my mouth..."

~ "De Profundis" by Georg Trakl

---

[2] The purely figurative and symbolic term "lepers" refers to multi-layered poems with cores of thematic complexity that deserve special regard, as well as extra care and attention, so as to be intellectually embraced for ideal understanding.

Musemagik

According to my writer-friend Magda…
her muse
wears an ethereal, cascading veil
sparkle of star
silken plume of quail
This muse
speaks in sparrow
and murmurs
in dialect of dove
cautioning her
that His rainbows are but mirage
"See" she whispers
(not in language of man)
"how they melt
in Mother Nature's mouth of rain…"

A Lady
of silent intensity:
a telepathic banshee
(of unseen beauty)
who flails her arms and voice
in a blood jet of ideas…
The fingers of her muse
death's-head
moths
fluttering under her skin,
Magda's soul again and again
awakens to the abrupt arrival,
feeling like—
a cobra
facing a mongoose
whose fur stands on end
as it lunges—
The only truth
bleeds from that moment

into…
her…
pen…

Swill o'Swain

Ghostly chorus
(*Coraline*)
fairies-swirl-the-niiiight

I grab a pen
& paper and then
resolve to
"Get black on white"
(Merci, Guy de Maupassant!)

And so the feelings float
like feathers:
Swansdown
in my brain
…Ebony head,
eyes of red
thrill of "ink & quill"
to quell TECHtime
(the buzzkill)

…Who says Poetry is dead?

Thistlethink

Thistlethink:
touch the prickly pink
and stem of green
--an absinthe
to nudge
the brain to the brink

Green Fairy floating
sucre aflame
cloud of *louche*
opalescence
Maignan's "Green Muse'"
calls my name...

Fancy slotted spoon
lies corpse-like on lace,
a quill-less pen
is hugged exquisitely
by digits demi-numb

Close my eyes
to recapture
the original ink-iced
nature image
that will make the
word-waterfall come

Cotillion Eye Glinting Down

The scythe of earth
hangs like a hammock
between *cenicitas* ("little ashes")
to shimmy like a shark
~lythe phallic symbol: breathing
inside the tapestry-rose
lining of the executioner's mask:
he filled the guillotine
with bloodblisters of stars
until a Spanish galleon
of "Blue Gato Delong"
ghostly lit
the spectral trail
of Packard-Mustang-Chevy
corpse-cars

Singing trees
like rain
dredge the air
with leaf-lyrics
and unchidden children
screech
like parrots:
Where are their piratical parents
to Jolly Roger
them into a sirensong
of silence?
To chatter, nay,
like a Fauvist parrot,
but to float sirenly and serenely
on a patina-pond
as a Monet waterlily
sprouting from Gala's
unsevered, unbloodied
eye socket
of Emporda

Thoughts trickling before sleep

(Part A) :

Greenswanic
swooning
impulses
ebb
into my heart's egress
into an estuary
that flows
into a
smilewide
glittersea
of me

(Part B):

Papal...pope-al
capsules
of light
meeting in a
Japanese confluence
in the chapels
behind my limbo-
letting eyes
~ *seppuku* ~
smiles
at me

Self As Sea

Loama shared
her night-dream
with flair--
this is exactly what she said to me...

"Panoply of Penelopes
in a pinkshell
halcyon of me...
shards of stained glass
prick my veins:
my blood runs red
then black again

There's a whore on the shore
but I don't recognize
her gown of cesspool
or her resemblance to me...
...shell of a showwoman
who has lain her wordwhip
down near the broken
shards of shells

Strains of conch-welk-scallop-coral
sunlight
stream Stradivariusly
as I am awakened saltily
by a soul-tsunami
of tears"

Swan Junket

Day Mary,
swinging on the moon's cusp
riding glitter
'til the sun's eyelids (bronzepink)
open—wide in worry
for the world below:

Toiling in its oil
of circular swirls
rainbowed by
water spirits
sent from the sky
to purify the rancid…

(but the crystal of rain is in vain)

Day Mary
climbs the
silver-runged
ladder of stars
to reach the blue velvet
apex of the sky
~her diving platform
is of air
as She arrows through
stratus,
cumulus,
nimbus
to land as a feather
~cloud-soft and ethereal~
in the captain's seat

Confidently, she commandeers
…the plump
of plush
red velvet
to steer
this swan junket
over the rainbow

Taproot

Brushing slowly a cascade of titian tresses aside, Livia, her eyes the hue of beryl, sat attentively next to Jude who meaningfully clasped her hand, and gushed a vision of 6-winged seraphim communicating to God in a divine deluge--Just as his Muse communicated with him, he explained.
...And then another waterfall of words to make her truly understand:

        Tap
        into
        root:
gush of mystery
   darksap
   of shades
    honey
   of heresy...
brown braids
   of bark
   twining
    like
    veins
    amok
burly banyans...
throbbing members
   in dirt
  rain-drunk
with Mother Nature's
   purity
and bittersweet
   nectar
  of being...

Tree-tranquility
  is torn
by blue sky
  criers...
...starlings
 careening
through leafy arms
 screeching
 at the sun

Lovecrest

Stretching to meet
him in blueshale shadows
black lines
chalky edges
~dimension
dalliances
as I swallow
the pale
parading
as Fauvist ovum
in Paul Klee-eyes
He whispers
in melted syllable
as my mouth
fragments
like bullets--
--or butterflies
…only to regroup
in disjointed
dove-flock…
To stab,
to gel
like shards
of shale
chalky blue:
I breathe crooked
on Cubist cue

Chameleon under a Black Rainbow

Chameleon crouches under a lotus-laced rainbow
        which is melting…
Butterfly flits wryly by
        (the dilettante eternal)
Ladybug limps out of Hell
        then is eaten by Diamondback
        (the debutante infernal)
Wolverine sniffs the amber sky
        Night is fast falling
Her mate is calling calling:
        but she ignores him and sashays away
        …far away
She-wolf nudges the man-skull with her paw:
        the smile is a crooked row
        of sun-bleached teeth
        the eye-sockets are empty / dark as sin
        She trots away, a grey silhouette
        in the ethereal cobalt-blue of dusk
--salvation is the snow on the mountain beyond

  Now chartreuse,
        Chameleon lounges under a black rainbow;

  Now obsidian, the skull smiles
        Chameleon lashes her tail like a whip,
        hurtling the skull
        into the jungle river

  Piranha swims through the skull's eye-sockets
        She is ravenous

Bloom-of-the-Womb

He said: She is an iris —
    misunderstood and a slave
    to the soil of my touch…

    Yet…

coal to diamond   sand to pearl
drop to ocean   sapling to oak
baby to girl…………………to Woman
    who
in her pomegranate spring
    revels
    rain-drunk
and green-veined…

Laughing, she shakes
    her leafy self
    and lifts
    her sanguine face
to Janus Cosmic's twilight sky:
soon she will be swallowing stars
    like the mouth of night

~ firefolk smoldering on her tongue ~

    Her sister, The Iris
    is a delicate messenger
    (noble *sufrida*)
    bruised purple
    by his thorny words
    ~curled petals

    shriveled
by the sun of her phoenix-soul
where rebirth is roseruddy
    survival is rootright

Blood Bloom

Nestled in my muse
of *matryoshka*
are minds
of minutiae
souls
in motes of light
voices
singing
from the mouths
of unblinking doll faces
who wear babushkas
of varying shades
the verity of vermillion
~all looking (and feeling)
as true…as wondrous…as resilient
as heart-harkening
as red
as Stein's rose
Standing in the warmth of rank and file
…these Women
petal-pained…
…yet stem-strong and leaf-lively
together
lift their smiling faces
skyward
to share-as-one
the corolla
of the sun

Abby & Me: A.D.

White sulky smoke mingles with the motley mob
at 180 RPMs the music pumps
as the lashing lights incite
a techno-orgy
Fools' Delight

(Coo Androgyny Purr Decadence)
hepcats in skullcaps
boors in berets
sluts in sausage curls
drones in dreads
boys in bull nose-rings
-all in sync-
as Duessa the Whore of Babylon in a babydoll dress
of blackest velvet
in classic "HELLegance" performs her dance of deception:
Marron Judas-eyes mosh with the mob
as her Black Widow-body
convulses to the primal beat
her black, suede clogs scuttle like scorpions as…
two male admirers, inextricably
swaddled in her lipsticky web,
are tethered by her smile, as they too, join in
the dance (of delusion).
"O my pretty ones"
she lilts, laughing canyon-mouthed
as the 3-headed cocoon raves on
~~Marlene Dietrich Incarnate

II
Like the fools in Her Court
who are cloaked by the Cosmic Cobweb,
the gyre is slimy with Time
slippery in its spiralscape to oblivion
as one lone girl
my brethren
is up Against The Wall
We are not sister to Duessa the sooty-black dahlia
or Cinderella the starry-eyed

coquette in glass stilettos
We are siblings to rags, ashes
and smashed pumpkins…
With long honeyspun tresses
that lie limp against her 70s-style striped turtleneck
she sits in smoky silence, cross-legged in bellbottoms
peering through Coke-bottle specs…at Them
looking aloof,
--but what WE are (is Shy)
Together we are origami
steeling
our paper-prism souls
against the tsunami
of the spiritual mosh pit;
in survival mode,
we ignore the Gumbyesque commotion
--determined not to break
and nonchalantly
peer
at each other
in soulspeak
wrapped…rapt
in our own
warm webs
of solitude…
~Greta Garbos Incarnate

Giana in the Wheat

Hiding
in Demeter's Bosom
crouches Giana
--so dark
against the undulating sea of amber
Long-lashed and saucer-eyed
she spies
through the windwhip
on an August day
an elephantine oval
~~cookie-cut precision
by a silversprawl of lightmass
that vanishes in an eyeblink…

Hand to mouth,
Giana darts home--steamrolling wheat in her wake
to tell Mami and Papi…that God has stepped foot in the field
"No *nina*" they scold gently,
"…only boys tell tales"

On the evening news,
the grey-suited anchor man
with a facial tic
calls the unexplained phenomenon a
"crop circle"

With the determination of a 7-year-old,
Giana says,

"No, it's a Godstep."

With the wisdom
of ancient blood
Mamacita replies,

"Si, cosa linda"

while wistfully
stroking her daughter's raven hair

Arinna

A succinct storyteller, Aunt Meadie, spun this wisp-o-wisdom tale of family gold for Cora Virginia, who dabbed her eyes, carefully folded up the paper on which it was written in flowing letters, and slid it into her dusty suitcase, which held the remnants of her (new) Old Life…scattered bones in the moonlight; the melancholy hue of a Valentine heart would be seeping soon…

>Arinna
>picks up the river
>trying to carry
>creativity and destruction
>with her.
>
>In the buckyard
>antlers parade
>jauntily
>against a turquoise backdrop.
>
>Then the deer seep
>into the jade-lit wood
>tracking teardrops
>of salt and silt.

Ruth

Grizzled old woman
in polyester pants
holding a grey pocketbook
like an albatross
around her pruney arm
her eyes are like blue chips
in a mud puddle.

She's at home now...
slipping into times more comfortable
her mantra, "Remember when?"
is a black pillbox hat she wears
to mourn yesterday
as she fingers black and white photos
while rocking
in her poodle-chewed chair:
How well she remembers
jitterbugging all night long
and stopping a car
with a flash of thigh
when she and best friend Nellie needed a ride
to the dancehall on Saturday night...

Now Nellie dances with angels
and Ruth's heart hangs
like a pendulum
ticking with memory

The sun ducks behind a hill
as gnats truck[3]
merrily around the bug-light on her front porch
Glen Miller's "Moonlight Serenade"
crackles from an old record player

---

[3] Truck -A shuffling dance-step in the Jitterbug of the 1930s and 1940s

In pearls and rouge,
she waits for the Tall Dark Stranger;
a crescent moon glints
in her faded, blue eyes

~~the rocking stops
With pearly-pink lips, Ruth smiles in welcome
~~She has promised him the Last Dance for years now

Burnt Offering

I am a statue
of marble
created to mark
a time of glory for Man
~~a time of warring winds
and indifferent rains
The sun
is a smiling sculptor
who etches lines
with his fingers
on my stoic
face-façade
In my moonward darkness
tears have sweat
from my insides
to form a pool of pity
about to dynamite
this dam-damn(ed)
~but then I'd be nothing
but another fallen ruin
(forgotten rubble and faceless dust)
~but then I guess
the sun-sculptor
has known this, as every season
with strokes
of airiest gold
he has touched me
(scarred me)
so the swans
stare unkindly now
Then the fairies dance feverishly
in a ring
of noonday flame: vermillion-jacinth-xanthous
around me…
Stoically sunward
I am still a statue
ever-shadowed by Time
when they collapse
near the melted sundial

MoonMince

Cresting the sun
besting the one
only to be palsied by
fingers of crevice
allowing me
the Cicada
--no entrance

(although I've left hope unattended)

like Kennedy roses
forlorn
and aware
of their thorns
~for eons of the soul

Whittle me white
Don Death

your quixotic charms
as hypnotic as the green light
ethereal
above a corpse
still
soul-hazy from your kiss…

MoonMince
haven't seen the sun since

…the No Exit sign
shines on

My Butterflies After Midnight

Black-tipped
indigo and powdery magenta,
they wing into the world
~boudoir bombers~
when a bedroom window gapes open
wayfarers of the world
when spring yawns into being:
chrysalis-christened,
but nay, imprisoned
they eventually shimmy on
tides of air
ever-ebbing
towards the island of the moon:
night's silvery sun
fluttering to alight
on color-caressed flowers
and alabaster
fingers
Such naturists
do not terrify
like Dali's locust
or mystify
like Frost's spider
…these insect-angels
gracefully
kamikaze
into karma
~inspiring
us to believe:
We too
can fly

He
to J. & S.

He dynamites the envelope
(to diamond bits)
pushing consciousness forward
punishing the banal
with lapis-blue looks
-pupils of black pearl-
that pierce outward
and inward

Yet he
is a human pincushion
enduring acupuncture
de coeur
--stab after silversweet stab
His soul slumps in the sweatbox
to him, Love is...
salivating on the bit
Yet he longs to feel
windkiss moonwan
and refuge from She
(his tigress-eyed keeper)
who towers above him laughing
cloud-crowned
jingling
the keys to the queendom
and his freedom

He who has placed his heart on a platter...knowingly
now lies to himself to live
denying
that he will never escape
the infamy
of dying every day
as
Salome's
Mojo

Posies and Pyres

Stubble-studded
Nero
rotting in his cell
surrounded by the soul-stench
of yesterday;
memories of charred eyes…melting jawlines
his darkly dancing
Cinderella
screaming
with every kiss
of flame
…magnificently combusting
into a burnt bouquet,
a ring of rose-wet ashes.
He laughs as he puffs
on a smuggled smoke
A run-in with Raoul
in the corner of the courtyard
almost costs him
his coveted "coffin nail."
One black eye later
(for Raoul)
he smokes
the courtyard, the barbed wire fences,
the steel bars and the green virgin
grass outside of the prison
away
in a daydream

Affixed to his lip like
a bony growth
his cigarette pulses with every puff
as he eavesdrops on the nearby cluster
of Lifers
who reminisce about blood
blades   bullets…
breasts…milky skin…mocha skin
--angels without wings

Jonah from Cellblock 3
knows Jesus

(claims he found him in the courtyard one day)
He's been trying to introduce

Nero
to J.C. for a while now…
Nero yawns
As Jonah yammers on
--a brand of the cross
glaring from his forehead:
"Brother, thy flesh is weak;
you must purge thy sin…"

He then points urgently
to a passage
in The Bible:
Isaiah saw a vision
of an angel, six-winged,
hovering near the light
blazing
from God's throne

The seraphim cached a burning coal
whale-mouthed
in glorious sin-singe
enough to short-out
the golden circuitry of heaven

Nero blinks
pauses
then sears
his own pale wrist
Liddy-like

--Jonah winces
Laughing, Nero
flicks his lit cigarette at him
and strides away
--a headcase with ashes
for a soul

Kaiser Kiss

In a pilgrim-style pinafore
she strides in
with a Hitler strut
and bleached-blonde
mustache
Her Eichmann eyes tiny
swastikas of blue
--As Heidi
sprawled out
in red poppies
--as Gretchen
begrudging gruel
to orphans
with pasty faces
and sunken eyes
…flat brown
as a cat-retched mouse

Out of the atomizer-fogged Ladies' Room
she propels herself
like a newborn
Nazi
hair twined in ropes
brassy nooses

In hose and heels
she is resurrected…
electric skeleton>
 < pearlsticky flesh…

as she sweats & frantically
goose-steps
on the light-sliced dance floor
and then —
The STRIKE
of the heil-hand
breaking
carnival glass
of our once-peaceful sky

Satori in a Bell Jar

Lithium is his elixir
he savors its flavor
bitterness is sweet salvation
every day he does the slugslide
on his front porch
to walk *Precious* the poodle
--his only friend with a pulse—
save his weasel-faced mama
his personal Madonna
who squints and scowls, squints and scowls
under the scrutiny of the sun

Pre-Lithium, he howled at the moon
charged into our front yard
threatening and thrashing
At gunpoint he was pried from our property
by humble saviors in blue;
still snarling, the bloated Dahmer clone
(my next-door neighbor)
was caged that night
After being tranquilized,
the sullen seether
was questioned by a psychiatrist
In my neighbor's razored mind's eye,
He was Quasimodo and I was his La Esmeralda

Neither strait jackets nor the legal system
could hold him
Now mother and son share the same
disease: Denial
When he sits on his porch in a slugslump
rocking lethargically,
does he ever see the light
…know *satori*?
Or is he forever locked in limbo
(with his professed best friend Freddy Krueger)
trawling for tomorrow
and secretly slouching
closer to our door

Honkytonk Heartbreak

Just around sunset...
with coyote eyes
they prowl into town
slinking gray

With vulture hearts
they swoop into town
to pounce on prey squeezed into denim
--victims are like cowskulls in the desert:
calico roses bloom through
the eye-sockets

Wearing dirty snakeskin boots
hung with silver, strutting
with clodhopper cadence
cowboys saunter into town;
even dust is phallic...

With dust-encrusted bravado
their ten-gallon hats
prod the blue-bruised sky
(She watches and aches overhead)
Cracked, leather-faces crowned with crows' feet,
circle around and with a YEE-HA
and a "Howdy-do Little Darlin's"
they close in to pluck two hothouse flowers
(in babydoll dresses)
dripping with blue roses
who have sprouted long, curly hair as soft
and white as milkweed

(Leigh and Mandy have both endured
this ilk of cowboy for far too long;
a pitcher of poison would be less painful
than the tongue-rattle of their lies
and the icy vise of their rough touch)

The ladies feign surrender
with a smile, wilting on cue
...with man-branded souls
their spirits have been broken
one time too many--
in a spaghetti (strap) Western;
even cowgirls get revenge

Two Camel cigarettes ringed in red
smoothly ground into the dust
as together they savor Cheshire cat smiles at Cowboys

"One of these days our boots
are gonna stamp
you PAID — Long Due"

Mandy and Leigh
revise on-key
while
slipping
last-minute
necessities
into dress pockets:
Money
lipstick
cigarettes
scorpions

~ tangoing in a trinket box ~

danse macabre
is on their minds

Calico Roses in a Skull Vase

Hiding in the butter
yellow of the desert
he wants to slither
through striations
of sand
undetected - invisible
feel the heartbeat
of the sand quickening
and his own resolve thickening
Though by nightfall he'll wish to
be eating the lizard's gizzard
and his own heart out
for leaving her at the
train station
knowing she would all
but sink down
(head like a rain-bent flower)
to the platform in despair
her long, obsidian-black tresses
cascading onto her tear-wet face
when she realized that he had pushed her into
a golden quicksand of lies
mirage of promises
…and the vultures, stark & dark
glinting
in the sun-squint
keep circling overhead
waiting patiently
for the melting man
to become carrion
so they can pick
his bones clean

Moon's Metal

Silver[4]
  slides down
    my neck
      cuddles my collarbone
       encircles my finger
       stabs my earlobes
      to hang
       vaingloriously
        for all to see
         Diana's minion
          cool mirrored metal
          glinting
           in a mater's nightlight
           bewitching humans
           with its beauty by day
           toppling moonbeasts
           in mid-howl
           with its fatal touch by night…
         --Lulling
        such
        lycanthropes
       to a sterling demise
       as its mother
      ~eternal Eye of Night
     gazes
    down
   approvingly

---

[4] *Moon's metal* - "silver" in the book <u>Many Moons</u> by Diana Brueton

Gypsy Crescendo

Shedding the cloak
of His Society
the usurper enters
their cloistered camp with caution
amid the primal music…
the wanton dancing by flickering flames
of jacinth
warming jackals
Ebony eyes glitter
taunting him with
Freedom he will never feel…
Power he will never possess…
Magic he will never master

Lascivious laughter seemingly mocks
the outsider
as he throws down
a bag of silver
before the wizened fortuneteller
(her face is a pitted pearl
her smile, a crescent moon)

Impatiently drumming his fingers on the table,
he smugly waits for confirmation
of a honey-coated future:
What He Richly Deserves

Studying his anemic face
hollow, jade eyes
and condescending smirk
--visibly whitewashed
even
in the palsied candlelight
she knows
that it will be too easy…

Her swarthy, bejeweled fingers
caress the crystal ball
-as if-
to coax Fate to answer;

the *gaje** gluts himself on the clandestine crime
of tethering time
proffering his sickly soul to the darkness
as a (self-described) minx in the mist
cackles jovially...

A shadow slides
ominously across the moon
eclipsing the silver of the skycoin
then with a limeslice smile
the wise gypsywoman speaks
the language of shadow:

Skummade igenom[5]
        limp back

goat-footed
        to your whited sepulcher

of existence
        and beware

of jackals
        skulking in the dark wood

--they also go your way

His pale face erupts
in erubescence
like a blood drop
on a white rose
as her shameless eyes shimmer

---

[5] *gaje = "outsider" in the Romany language
*Skummade igenom = "white man from town" in the Romany language

L'oncle-In-Law

I…know…you, sir:

Semi-staid statue
monument in motion
…but with icy innards
a "pill" of a community pillar

True, you've traveled the world
(France, England, Africa, Spain)
you openly share
your cornucopia of knowledge
about different cultures
you fluidly speak
many languages
--but you cannot communicate--

At family gatherings
when mothers, children, fathers, nieces, nephews, cousins
all sit and chat in circles
of warmth
--linked by untimed smiles
I cannot help but feel your contempt
coiling around me
like an invisible cobra
with forked tongue
w<u>HISS</u>pering
words of venom

The bite is a scar
a reminder that War
is not always a
bitter struggle between strangers
On every holy holiday…and backyard bbq
you have sought me out
with verbal daggers
~~uncloaked for all to know

The truth, dear sir, is
that you are only
a Medusa
-head to me now;

I turn away
to avoid
your piercing eyes
as your sharp words
once again
fall jagged
like inverted teardrops
of stone

Pere Heirs

"Come, let's mix
where Rockefellers
walk with sticks
or um-ber-ellas
in their mitts…"
"Puttin' On The Ritz" ~~Taco

Mother

Sucre

Soeur

Swine

…In a glitter

of

!@#$ DIN $#@!

they

dine

Echoes of Adam

During coffee & conversation, my writer-friend Dahlia
described to me the current state of the world
in her characteristic poetic way:

Aged angels
sitting on blue marble
stoops
counting stars
gathering snowflakes
~eco-eggs
that fry
melt
in the nuclear horizon:
A red numb of nimbus
reverberates
in silence…
radiates from the holocaustic
heat
of its
dead
mother
whose son-flock
of atom // adam
chose to eat of
the shiny red
apple
after all

Peck…peck…poof!

…and then a bit more coffee and conversation,
before we had to leave
the warmth of words,
the comfort of caffeine,
the emotional coziness
of the café behind.

Black Lily: A Slight Incantation

Black Lily
--a bur in my soul
parasite of hope
will suck me whole

Field of wheat
field of stone
river of blood
valley of bone

Hell to the hilt
ye wither, ye wilt
thou root thyself
in a hole of hope
(no soil, no sun)
just a vine of rope

Wisteria of hysteria
worm-winding wounds
in the father-fertile

    d
    a
    r
    k
    n
    e
    s
    s

of Mother Earth's womb

Breezy Green Limbo

Lolling in the great spaces
steeling
against the slate faces
waiting for the leavening
passage
to paradise
away from pain
on earth
to the great grainy
beyond…
…rising warmly
above me
as I notice
(to my surprise)
that through the wormholes
of my ribcage
sprout not milkweed
heads of promise
but the ever-winding
coil
of ivy
--Its color
quickening
as I weaken
to wisdom

London Son

London son
so fog-found
and crumpet-
crushed
by the lace of light
silently coiling
from the belltower
~cyclops eye
a stare…
(the voyeur's voyage)
sloshes on
My soul
is his first mate
floating on and in
an icefloe
in the sea
of our heart chambers
--Where be the axe
to butcher
us out
of this
clearsolid prism?
-prison-
I am wilderness:
wolves howling, wind wailing
mountains bracing
for Winter's eyeblind
whitelash of snow…

Feel me breathe in sun
as I am glacially glistening
melting in his smile
as golden light
laces down
the face
of Big Ben

Banshee Breeze

Banshee breeze
wailing through
speciously-splayed trees
careens
       banefully
invisibly
      --shamelessly
bemoaning a tale
of impending grief

Woman-wind of Woe
Pain-monger
flailing through fragile planes
once a throbbing
trinity
of heart, body, and soul
now haunts Irish humans
namelessly
--her voice
an unforgettable
tremor
sharding the night
(reverberating with no rest)
--her truth
a forewarning
of Death's palsied coming
for a loved one
--her tortured spirit
a timeless testimony
to the orphans of fortune
still begging to be heard

An Iris View

Segua seeks the unique;
the tweaks and freaks of humanity:
to her, the insanity of everyday life
is a vanity
not a calamity
to sob about
or feel robbed about
She is a struggling actress
who rents a rainbow for a day
(no receipt, or guarantee, of course)

Her son Adam
is the apple of her periwinkle eye;
she, his angel-mama, in thriftshop threads

"Color…let's color, Mummy…"

She reaches for a broken puce
and a stubby magenta

*"No, mum – those are nimrod's crayons…
pick these"*

With a melancholy smile,
Segua tousles his towhead
and in her liquid lilt
of scotch and soda
says simply:

"Love, sometimes
the ugly ones
are best"

IDiotica

*To those who choose to mildew
in Dilbertian cubicles:*

A lilybyte
to languish
on the pond electric…
a scent of sense
more potent than sensamilla

A cyberslug
to thwart this thug
(sunnyday mongers)
~the bug in their mind-melded brains
<> automatons in the Grendel-grip of groupthink <>

Conformity is their wobbly crutch
when they
in fool's cap & bells
limp pain
-fully into the center ring
to disappoint

The Suit…The Boss
their grimacing grey-faced ringmaster
/ lash after lash /
~then to see their own grey, gaping
Edvardian faces
in the mirror

Filmmakers

Eggshell esoterica
enshrouds itself
cerebrally
as He peers quixotically
at an angular coffin
chalky lines
of cobalt and plum...

...She is propelled
by her perennially flowering
storyboard
through a dahlia-dark tunnel
of tiny, tinny sound
and sorrow o' morrow
water — drip drop
stalagmite stalagtite

Ideas
firmly formed
can be icicles of purity:
I wonder...

will
they
pierce
gently
or
wound
fat(e)ally
with

i
m
p
u
l
s
e
?

Digital Swan

A flash
of feathers
slices
up sunlight
into an airy mosaic
above the lake-
as-mirror

A swan swims
in a current
of wind
as wings lash
a line of Ledas
for being open
like a corolla
of a rose,
and closed
like the mouth
of a stone

Backwards,
the swan
white-as-winter
but as warm as the Everglades
glides
on glass
strangely dotted
with breadcrumbs
(no Hansel or Gretel to be found)
as the sun sinks
into the pink
flame-of-flamingo
horizon
…Pan's pointillism

La Danse de Vie

Spinning in an inward spiral
unclothed
naked in that cosmic ballroom:
hungry eyes
feast
vampirically
on your vulnerability...
laughing lovelies
drink
in the sight
of your dahlia-delicate skin
and sense
your milk & silk soul...
as if it were smilingly smooth
kahlua & cream
(or a thicker, warm concoction)
In the daze
of days
Dance On
existentialist ballerina
twirling 365
...24-7
on the slippery
--yet pretty, pink lid
of Pandora's box

And then **Coralyn** *awoke*
from her delicious – dark dream
her pen pirouetting
black on white
ink flowing
like
kahlua
in cream
to record
her mantic mind's
musing

Cantomine

Splash of wine
on pristine orchids…
cackles of laughter
as I "take the air"
to clear my mind,
to let an old/new thought take root…
Field of gold
like fire
furtively
blazes up
with indifference
against my chafed
knees
my mosquito-bitten
thighs
~wheat the color
of a lion's mane
paled by the sun
undulates creamily
under the wind's
unmistakable embrace
and I sit apart
from nature
human nature
as a dark dahlia
ashen yet airy
smoldering
in an invisible garden of isolation
(away from the chatty, boozy book club perched
on the mint julep-of-a-porch)
~reliving
the same flames
of social pilgrimage
~feeling the inferno of alienation
that I know
so well

MetroGnome

"...*a bobolink has pins. It shows a nail.*
What is a nail. A nail is unison... "
~"Susie Asado" by Gertrude Stein

O Yilth
to the lessermost
to the glistening
gutterboast
[see] banomion
[say] buh-NO-myun
hail hale
and hearty gnome
weighted
whisper
of pitiless
pendulum
dust-dervish
and din
of hippodrome

PALE---PaLe---pale

palindrome

...Alaska's

PALIN = DRONE

Blue Room, Red Room[6]

"In the blue of an electric dawn...the water lilies bend and break."
~Henry Miller, <u>Tropic of Cancer</u>

Crowned in a wedding veil
of rose-point lace
Jacqueline Bouvier
never wanted to be
Guinevere
in that dubious Camelot:
She was a pearl
among swine
-Bay of Pigs-
While on TV
she gracefully showed
the nation
Lincoln's bed and Washington's bust
...her husband viewed
both of Marilyn's...
Behind the mist
and jeweled sky
of the backdrop
(the First Lady was last on his list)
Yet for her kingdom,
she was Dignity
Incarnate
instinctively reaching
for the piece of her husband
that a stranger's bullet
had torn asunder...
In this bloody eye
of a national hurricane
Zapruder captured
Lady Zeitgeist
on film

---

[6] The poem's title is taken from the names of two rooms on Jacqueline Bouvier's historic and comprehensive White House Tour in 1962. *Rose-point lace:* Jacqueline Bouvier Kennedy's actual wedding veil was made from her grandmother's rose-point lace.

Revelation

While witnessing an ashen blue sky
that waxes from lavender to orchid
a Mother Goose moon
hangs unwavering in the west
~Nightlight of Nature~
He blinks, glassy-eyed,
Gothic darkness
cloaks the orchid
panorama…
the inky ooze
of a vampire's cape swathing a victim
with cordial cruelty
juxtaposed…atop
the peach and purple rose
majesty
of a Victorian sunset:
jacinth embers
braided with holyhope
to hand a burning rope
(strange strength)
to the awestruck witness
who feels the terminal tug
of "dark night of the soul"
for the first time…
…Air and angels weight equally
at this moment
as tiny fingers tenaciously clutch
a soft teddybear at bedtime,
the boy's Candidian eyes gazing
at a Mother Goose moon
surrounded by a sackcloth sky

A Woman's Face

Morning is unkind
to a woman's face...
neither a splash
of lukewarm water
nor a dab of cool
cream can fill up the tiniest trenches
that He has dug
birthday-after-birthday
around the mouth
(smiles and frowns)
spaded
by sunrise and sunset
--or ragged ravines
etched on the forehead
by a mixed bouquet
of expressions
--or those two familiar gashes
between brows
that appear as bamboo-thin pen strokes
of an unfinished Chinese character
-sliced parallel-
by the blithe swing
of His Scythe

...Eve-flesh is never
cleansed,
soothed,
or reborn
like a calla lily
doused
by the stamen of rain:
O Yes,
Morning is unkind
to a woman's face

To Think Askance

Linsel-lock
Hansel-mock
The fist—
answered
see only lichen
on a rock…
I see together
I see alone
I see a time-pocked
face
of moss and stone
the eyes, butterflies
that alight
airily
in sunsteps of
frozen flight
the caterpillar of a mouth
forms a smirksmile
the "eyes" blink
blithely in a
woodland while…
…Knights of ashes,
damsels of dust,
unqueen the king
who's pawned the dawn:
once a honeyed horizon
now just powdery rust
sprinkled in a twinkle
on Monarch
butterfly wings…
C'est vrai, I see together
C'est vrai, I see alone
Resurrecting the magic
in web-delicate
fairy bones

Eyes Flashin' Ashen

Rain cranes its amorphous
neck to see:
Anhinga, the snake-bird
ashblack with wings
outspread
vampirically
holding back the wind as
I hear the breezy breath
of soul-pain in the leaflorn trees
(Seagrape, Umbrella)
The hummingbird
windspinner wobbles
in the windspan
wingspan of violence
as the wind chimes
plead plaintively
for peace and resolution
(A *"Bells for Her"*[7] tinkling)
Anhinga…phoenix…ashes
palm fronds look like a bendy straw
stretching, reaching
poised for a piece o' peace
(perfection)
Nature's nirvana
is not my pebble to plop/ feather to drop
or egg to perch atop
…It is a distant swan lake-locked yet
paddling kaleidoscopically towards me in 3-D
Stradivarius strokes of sunrise…
my coda of *cognitive disinhibition*
swims blackswanically
in a Rockette-line
of mirror reflections
upon
reflection
upon-

---

[7] "Bells For Her" by Tori Amos from <u>Under The Pink</u>, 1994

Anomalily[8]

To say the lady is Dark
is to say that she
hides a half-leaden soul
--the other half is burnished silver
She has led
herself through
cobwebbed voices
and false beacons
gossamers of light
in the labyrinth
Outside
in the wash of light
she dances
free
in the floribundas
then lies down in the bed
of freckled stargazer lilies
Her heart is the blue balloon
(let go by a child)
that floats past
the paintpot sun
into the indigo skycanvas
melding two worlds
But she knows that ephemeral things
are sometimes split
like skulls…
a shred of popped balloon
drops to the earth near the sea of lilies
where her soul is an island
Here a shred of sky serves
as a windborne monument
--a bluefaded
megalith
to the busy inhabitants
of an anthill
coolly shaded
by dahlias

---

[8] *Anomalily* is a neologism: anomaly + lily

About The Author

Originally from the woodsy warmth of a small town in the northern panhandle of West Virginia where she began writing creatively as a wee one in kindergarten, Gloria J. Wimberley, M.A., now lives with her husband and two children in South Florida where the eyeshine of gators is scant, but the sky-blue "plumage" of plumbago is plentiful.

As an <u>Edgar Allan Poet</u> scribe, Gloria also has had work published in *The Northern Virginia Review*, *Mothering Magazine* (under the pseudonym Mirandah Thorn), *Moondance Magazine*, *Muse Cafe Quarterly*, *Tapestry*, *Clockwise Cat*, *The Southern Ocean Review*, and various other print and online publications in the U.S. and abroad.

Wimberley has work included or forthcoming in the following anthologies: <u>*In The Company Of Women: An Anthology of Wit & Wisdom, Sass & Class*</u>, <u>*Mapping Me: A Landscape of Women's Stories*</u>, <u>*Return to Rural America: A West Virginia Anthology*</u>, and <u>*The Panty Drawer*</u>.

When not penning poetry, she teaches at Broward College in Ft. Lauderdale, Florida. <u>*Dialect of Dahlias*</u> is her debut collection of poetry.

You may follow the works of author Gloria Wimberley on her blog "***Dahlias.&.A.Chocolate.Typewriter***", at the following web address: http://www.dahlia-in-fl.livejournal.com/ You may also find her author-page on Facebook, and career profile on LinkedIn.

Acknowledgements:

- *Foreword and editing by Editor Apryl Skies, Co-editor Alicia Winski of Edgar & Lenore's Publishing House*
  ~ Los Angeles, CA

- *Sincere thanks to Sheenagh Fraley Rivera, Claudia Childress, Wanda Morrow Clevenger, Martin Willitts Jr., Annie H., Posy C. & James Brandolino for enriching my life with support and positivity.*

- *My LinkedIn connections for their support*

- <u>*World Literary Café*</u> *writers for their support*

- *Calliope's Closet: Celebrating Women's Literature and Artistry*

- *Edgar Allan Poet: Dedicated to preserving the integrity of poetics in art, culture and community*

- *Muse Café Quarterly*

- *Sparkbright Magazine*

- *The National Gallery of Writing*
  (sponsored by NCTE – National Council of Teachers of English)

- *LiveJournal – my poetry blog: Dahlias.&.a.Chocolate.Typewriter*

- *Moondance Magazine*

- *Poets OutLoud*

- *Bolts of Silk*

- *"The Empowered Mother" radio show by Amy Kovarick*

- *Mothering Magazine*

- *Literary Mama*

- *Clockwise Cat*

- *The Southern Ocean Review*

- *Tapestry*

- *The Northern Virginia Review*

- *Moonshade Magazine*

- <u>*Many Moons*</u> *by Diana Brueton*

- *Artwork & Photography from Dialect Of Dahlias; courtesy of Apryl Skies*

"The moon with its bandages ready to comfort the white
 creatures whose lips are torn by speech
Whose hair is the seaweed of the heart
Where the center of the ocean lies an unmarked grave
The songs of mermaids tumble out of the surf at midnight"
 --Pete Winslow, *A Daisy in the Memory of a Shark*

www.ingramcontent.com/pod-product-compliance
Lightning Source LLC
LaVergne TN
LVHW061216060426
835507LV00016B/1967